Before you begin

Read through what you have to do, and make sure you have everything you need.

If you are using anything messy like paint, glue or varnish, cover your work area with newspaper, and put on an apron.

Ask one of your parents which is the best place to do your project.

Be very care...

If you are using a knife, put the thing are cutting onto a flat surface to cut Keep your hands away from the blad

When you are using scissors always keep the points facing away from you.

Always put pins and needles away when you have finished using them.

If you use turpentine, put the top back on the bottle immediately. Wash your hands carefully when you have finished.

If you are cooking

Always ask an adult to help you before you start to cook.

Turn saucepan handles to the sides of the stove so that you do not knock them.

Always put on oven mitts before picking up anything hot or when putting things into or taking them out of the oven.

Be very careful when boiling things.

When you have finished

Wash your paint brushes and put the lids back on cans and tubes.

Clean and straighten everything up.

First published in 1985 by Usborne Publishing Ltd,
20 Garrick Street, London WC2E 9BJ, England
© 1985 Usborne Publishing
Printed in Italy

PARTY FUN

Clare Rosen
Illustrated by Lily Whitlock

CONTENTS

Series Editor: Angela Wilkes

Giving A Party

Guests
Matthew
Anna
Freddy
Jane

Games
Treasure hunt
—treasure
10 clues
Peas and straws
—peas
straws
cups

Food
cake
rolls
biscuits
ice cream
sausages

SHUT YOUR PETS IN A QUIET ROOM WHILE YOU ARE HAVING THE PARTY

If you plan your party well it will be really good. Send out the invitations about two weeks before the day.

Make a list of friends you want to ask. Count how many there are so you know how much of everything to make.

Then make a list of the games you are going to play and the things you will need for each game.

Get as many things ready as you can the day before the party. Make the cake and put it in an airtight can.

Before the party starts put a bunch of balloons on your door or gate so that your guests can find the house easily.

Themes

There are lots of different types of parties. If you choose a theme, make your invitation fit the theme (see page 4), and tell your guests what to wear. If the weather is fine, you could have an outdoor party, like a picnic or a barbecue, but you will need help from an adult.

Monster party

Make a monster pop-up invitation and tell your guests to look ugly! Make monster masks and brightly colored food.

Color party

Ask your guests to dress in one color, for example, yellow. Then make yellow streamers and lanterns. Dye the food with yellow food dye and make banana milk shakes.

Disco party

Put colored light bulbs in the lights and hold a disco dancing competition.

Zoo or Farm party

Draw animal faces on balloons. Make animal invitations and place names. Make a cucumber crocodile (see page 11).

Spooky party

Make ghost invitations and spooky decorations.

3

Pop-up Invitations

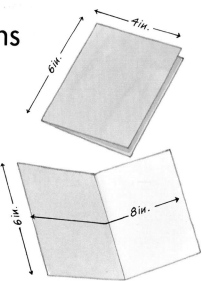

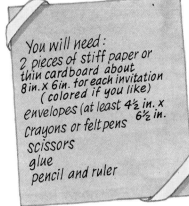

You will need:
2 pieces of stiff paper or
thin cardboard about
8 in. x 6 in. for each invitation
(colored if you like)
envelopes (at least 4½ in. x
6½ in.
Crayons or felt pens
scissors
glue
pencil and ruler

The picture inside the invitation pops up when the card is opened.

Fold two pieces of paper in half, crossways, as shown. One piece is for the card, the other for the pop-up.

To make the pop-up, fold one piece of paper in half again. Open it out, then cut out one quarter. Fold it in half crossways.

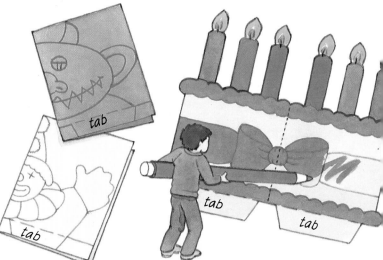

Draw half a cake against the fold. (You could draw any party thing like a clown or some balloons. Make it fit your party theme if you have one.) Leave a small space at the bottom of the paper and draw a tab on the bottom edge.

Cut out the picture and open it out. You will have a cut-out of a whole cake with two tabs on it. Color it in.

4

Open out the other piece of paper. Measure 2in. along the fold and make a dot. Draw lines across the card from the top corners through the dot to the other sides.

Fold the tabs on the cake back along the dotted lines, and put a little glue on the bottom of each one.

Stick the pop-up to the card so that the fold is in the middle of the card and the sides are along two of the lines, as shown. Press the tabs down.

Leave the glue to dry, then erase the pencil lines. Fold the card and draw a picture on the front.

On the inside of the card write the name of the guest, and when and where you are having your party. Write RSVP in the bottom corner. This means "Please reply."

5

Decorations

Chinese Lanterns

You will need:
brightly colored paper
6 in. x 10 in.
lantern
glue, tape,
scissors,
cotton thread

¾ in.

You can make a garland of lanterns by hanging some of them from a streamer.

Fold the paper in half lengthwise. Make folds ¾in. in along the long edges of the paper, as shown.

Open out the ¾in. folds. Cut strips about ¾in. wide where the dotted lines are in the picture, as far as the fold.

Streamers

You will need:
at least one packet
of crepe paper
tape
scissors

crepe

Keep the paper folded as it is in the packet.

Cut it into strips 2in. wide.

Run the scissors down both edges of the strips to curl them.

Unwind the strips and join them together with tape. Twist the streamers and stick them to the ceiling.

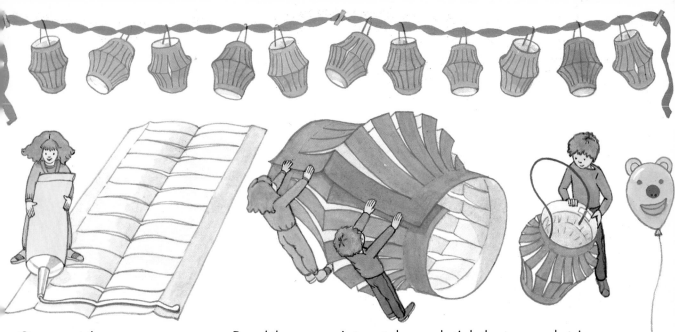

Open out the paper. Spread glue all along one of the end strips.

Bend the paper into a tube and stick the two end strips together. Stick a long piece of thread to both sides of the top edge with tape so you can hang up your lantern.

Decorated Balloons

You will need :
a packet of balloons
brightly colored paper
glue, scissors
felt pens, straws
string

Have enough balloons to give one to each of your guests when they leave.

Blow up the balloons. Cut out shapes, pictures or faces from the colored paper that fit the theme of your party.

Put a dab of glue onto each shape; then stick them onto the balloons. Tie a long piece of string to each one.

7

Masks

Masks are always fun at a party. Make one for each of your friends. They will have to guess who the other guests are. Make spooky masks for a Halloween party, ugly ones for a monster party and animal ones for a zoo party.

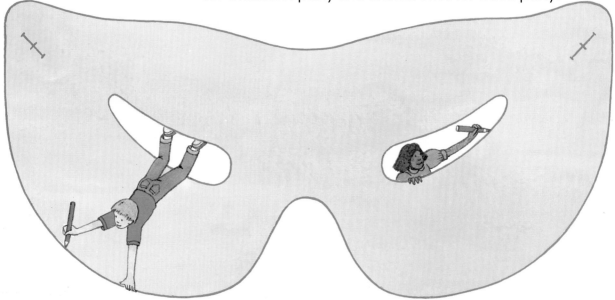

Use this pattern to make your masks. Trace it onto paper, then cut out the tracing.

Lay the tracing on a piece of cardboard and draw around it. Then cut it out carefully.

8

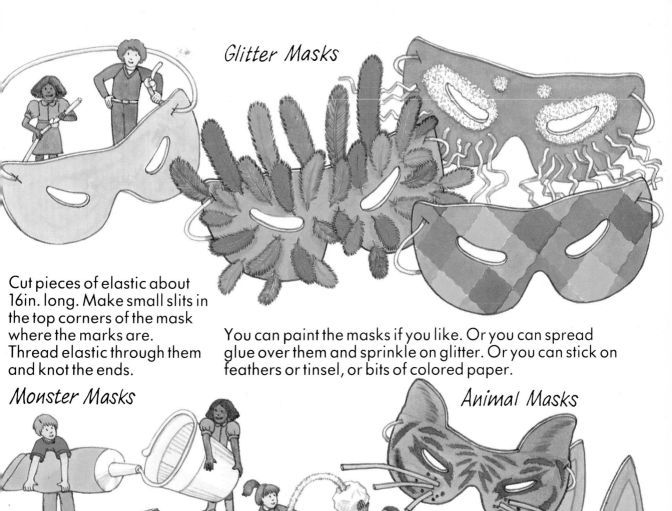

Glitter Masks

Cut pieces of elastic about 16in. long. Make small slits in the top corners of the mask where the marks are. Thread elastic through them and knot the ends.

You can paint the masks if you like. Or you can spread glue over them and sprinkle on glitter. Or you can stick on feathers or tinsel, or bits of colored paper.

Monster Masks

Cut holes in the bottoms of paper cups and glue them over the eye holes. You can make "feelers" by sticking pipe cleaners onto the backs of the masks with tape. Bend the ends over and crumple silver paper around them in balls.

Animal Masks

Paint the masks to look like animals. To make whiskers, glue straws on either side. Stick on paper ears.

9

Place Cards

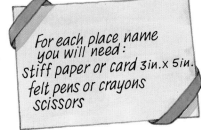

For each place name you will need:
stiff paper or card 3in. x 5in.
felt pens or crayons
scissors

Joe

Make place cards for all your guests to show them where to sit.

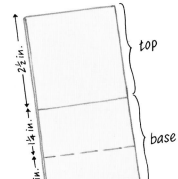

top

base

2½ in.

1¼ in.

1¼ in.

Fold the card in half. Fold one of the halves in half again. Open out the card.

Draw a simple picture on the top half of the card. Make it fit your party theme if you have one.

Kate

Tessa

Tom

Richard

Sarah

Jenny

Color in the picture with felt pens or crayons, then cut around it.

Bend the base back in half along the fold. Write the name of one of your guests on the base and stand the card on their plate.

Party Food

MAKE DELICIOUS LEMONADE OR COCOA FOR YOUR FRIENDS. MAKE SURE THERE IS ENOUGH FOOD FOR EVERYONE AND THAT IT LOOKS GOOD

sausages

chips

cookies

cheese crackers

hard boiled eggs

candy

toast fingers

carrot and celery sticks

grapes

Make open-faced sandwiches (see page 12), and a cucumber crocodile like the one below.

Fill bowls with chips and bite-sized things that people can eat with their fingers. Finish the treat with ice cream sundaes (see page 13) and a special cake (see page 14).

Cucumber Crocodile

You will need: a cucumber, small can of pineapple chunks, about 8 oz. cheddar cheese, two stuffed olives, 2 carrots, toothpicks

Make a slit in the fat end of the cucumber for a mouth. Make its eyes out of olives stuck onto toothpicks.

Make two holes at each end of the cucumber and stick short pieces of carrot in them for legs. Put cubes

of cheese and chunks of pineapple on toothpicks and stick them all along the crocodile like scales.

11

Snacks

Make delicious snacks with all sorts of different toppings, like these.

chopped egg and mayonnaise

peanut butter

cream cheese and date

cottage cheese and cucumber

cheese and tomato

liver pate

ham

egg and watercress

tuna fish

mashed banana

Take the butter out of the refrigerator a little while before you use it. It will be softer and easier to spread.

Decorate the sandwiches with fresh watercress, parsley or slices of lemon.

Ice Cream Sundaes

You will need:
ice cream, fresh fruit, canned peach halves plain chocolate, wafers, chopped nuts, candied cherries for decoration

Ice cream sundaes are made with ice cream, fruit, and sometimes sauce. Add a dollop of whipped cream if you like. Make them just before your party and keep them in the refrigerator.

skyscraper

Fill a glass with layers of ice cream and fruit, then top it with candied cherries.

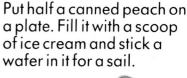

peach boat

Put half a canned peach on a plate. Fill it with a scoop of ice cream and stick a wafer in it for a sail.

chocolate sauce

Break 4oz. plain chocolate into the top of a double boiler with 3 tablespoons water. Heat it over hot water until it melts.

banana split

Put two scoops of ice cream on a plate. Cut a banana in half lengthways and stick the halves to either side of the ice cream. Decorate it with chopped nuts and grated chocolate, or pour chocolate sauce over it.

13

Party Chocolate Cake

You will need:

6 oz. unsweetened chocolate
6 tablespoons water
6 oz. butter or margarine
6 oz. soft dark brown sugar
4 large eggs
3 oz. ground almonds
3 oz. white bread crumbs
apricot jam

THE BOWL GETS VERY HOT. USE OVEN MITTS TO LIFT IT

Grease two 9in. cake pans. Set the oven to 375°F.

Melt the chocolate with the water in the top of a double boiler over hot water until it melts. Stir well.

Beat the butter in a bowl until it is soft, then beat in the sugar until it is fluffy.

Separate the egg whites from the yolks. You need two bowls. Crack each egg over one of the bowls, then slip the yolk from one half of the shell to the other. The white will slip into the bowl below. Put the yolk in the second bowl.

Beat the egg yolks, ground almonds, melted chocolate, and grated bread crumbs into the butter mixture.

DON'T OPEN THE OVEN DOOR BEFORE THE CAKE IS READY

Whisk the egg whites until they stand up in peaks. Fold them into the chocolate mixture with a metal spoon.

Spread half the mixture into each cake pan. Bake for about 20 minutes, until the centers feel springy.

When the cakes are cool, slip a knife around the sides of the pans and turn them out. Stick the two cakes together with apricot jam.

Icing

You will need:

3 tablespoons Corn Syrup
3 oz. butter
3 tablespoons cocoa powder

Melt the syrup with the butter over a low heat, then beat in the cocoa powder with a fork.

Beat the icing until thick, then pour it over the cake. Smooth it all around the cake with a knife.

Decorate the cake before the icing sets. If you are having candles put them firmly in holders.

Drinks

Fruity Milk Shakes

For eight guests you will need:

3 pints milk
1 lb. soft fruit
(e.g. bananas, strawberries)
or 10 oz.
can of fruit
(e.g. apricots, pineapple)
3 table-spoons sugar

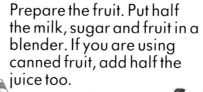

PEEL THE FRUIT AND TAKE OUT ANY PITS OR STEMS

Prepare the fruit. Put half the milk, sugar and fruit in a blender. If you are using canned fruit, add half the juice too.

Put the lid on firmly and blend for 30 seconds. Pour it into glasses. Blend the other half of the ingredients.

If you do not have a blender, mash the fruit with a fork, then whisk it into the milk.

Pour the milk shakes into tall glasses. Put straws in them. You can decorate the drinks with sprigs of mint or you could grate chocolate on top.

Fizzy Fruit Punch

For eight guests
you will need:

1 quart carton
unsweetened fresh
orange juice
1 quart lemonade
an apple, orange
and lemon
ice cubes
some sprigs of
mint

You should make fizzy fruit
punch just before your party
so the lemonade is still fizzy.

Wash the apple, cut it into
quarters and cut out the
core. Chop it up. Slice the
orange and lemon.

Put the fruit into a large jug
or bowl. Add the ice cubes
and mint.

Pour the orange juice over the fruit, ice and mint. Then add
the lemonade and stir everything gently together.

17

Indoor Games

Peas and Straws

For each player you will need:
a straw
2 cups
30 dried peas

Each player is given two cups. One is empty and the other has 30 peas in it.

Each player sucks the peas, one by one, onto the end of his straw and drops them into the empty cup. The first person to move all his peas into the second cup is the winner.

Eaties

For each player you will need:
a blindfold
a plate
10 different kinds of food (include things like dry cereal and spaghetti)

Put a bit of each kind of food on every plate.

Blindfold the players and give them all a plate of food. When they have eaten everything, take the plates away. Take off the blindfolds, so they can write down what they ate. The person to get most things right is the winner.

The Tray Game

You will need:
a large tray
about 20 small objects
pencils and paper

Put the things on the tray. Give your guests 3 minutes to look at it, then take it away.

The players must try to write down everything that was on the tray. The one who remembers the most things is the winne

Treasure Hunt

You will need:
10 small pieces of paper and a pencil
treasure (a small present or some wrapped candies)

First hide the treasure somewhere difficult to find.

Then write the clues on bits of paper. Each clue tells the players where to find the next clue. Hide the clues around the house. The last clue says where the treasure is.

Read out the first clue to everyone. Ask the players to put the clues back after they have read them. In this hunt, the first clue is—

1. I keep you dry— look in me for the next clue.

4. Monkeys love me— look under me for the next clue.

6. The next clue will come splashing out if you turn me on.

7. You dream on me— look under me to find the treasure.

2. I am soft and blue— look under me for the next clue.

5. You pick me up to stop me ringing— and find the next clue.

3. I light your bed-time story— look under me for the next clue.

The treasure is hidden under the bed.

19

Outdoor Games

Flowerpot Race

You will need:
- 4 plastic flowerpots
- 4 pieces of string at least twice as long as your legs
- scissors

To make the stilts, make a hole on each side of the flower pots with the point of the scissors, near the base. Pull a piece of string through the holes and knot the ends tightly.

The players stand in two teams. Put a marker about 10 yards from each team.

The first player in each team stands on the flower pot stilts, holds the string, walks to the marker, around it and back. He gives the stilts to the next player. The first team to all get around the marker and back wins.

Chocolate medals

You can give chocolate medals to the team who wins (see page 22).

Mailbox Game

You will need: 8 boxes, jars or cans
paper and a pen
tape
a table

Mailboxes

Rome
Paris
Athens
London
Bonn
Tokyo
Moscow
Lisbon

Letters

In this game the players must mail their letters in the right boxes – the Rome letter goes in the Rome box.

Write the name of eight capital cities on pieces of paper. Stick them to the eight boxes, jars or cans with tape. Hide the mailboxes around the yard.

To make letters, cut out eight small pieces of paper for each guest. There is one letter for each mailbox.

Write the name of one of the cities on each letter. Make a pile of letters for each player on a table.

Each player takes one letter at a time and writes his name on the back. Then he finds the right box to mail it in. When he has mailed it, he runs back for another letter. Check the boxes. The first player to mail all his letters is the winner.

21

Chocolate Medals

You will need:

chocolate (about ½ oz. for each medal)
small cupcake liners
a baking sheet, aluminium foil
paper ribbon (the kind you wrap presents with)

Give a chocolate medal to anyone who wins a game.

Melt chocolate in top of a double boiler over hot water.

Put the cupcake liners onto a baking sheet.

Pour melted chocolate into each liner, just covering the bottom. Leave the chocolate to cool and set.

Gently push the chocolate discs out with your thumbs and wrap each one in a piece of aluminium foil.

Cut a piece of paper ribbon about a yard long for each medal.

Stick a ribbon to the back of each medal with tape.

Presents

GIVE YOUR GUESTS A SMALL PRESENT AS THEY LEAVE. WRAP A LITTLE TOY OR GAME IN COLORED TISSUE PAPER OR WRAPPING PAPER.

Present Tree

In the summer you could hang the presents on a small tree or bush.

Tie a piece of yarn or string around each present and hang them from the tree.

Surprise Box

You will need:
a large cardboard box
crepe paper
a newspaper
small, wrapped presents

Cover a cardboard box with crepe paper. Fill the box with a jumble of presents and crumpled newspaper.

When the guests are leaving they can each dip their hand in and find a present.

Going Home Bag

You will need:

colored paper
string
tape
little presents
scissors
felt pens
old magazines

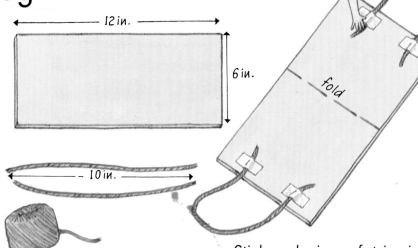

12 in.

6 in.

10 in.

fold

Make little bags for your friends to take home and fill them with tiny surprise presents.

Cut out a strip of paper 12in. by 6in. Cut two 10in. pieces of string.

Stick each piece of string in a loop at either end of the paper like this, to make handles.

Sophie

John

Daniel

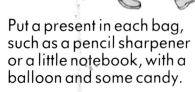

DON'T FORGET TO SAY "THANK YOU" WHEN YOU LEAVE A PARTY

Fold the paper in half. Stick the sides together with tape. Write the guest's name on it with felt pens.

Decorate the bag with felt pens or cut pictures out of magazines and stick them on. Make them fit your party theme if you have one.

Put a present in each bag, such as a pencil sharpener or a little notebook, with a balloon and some candy.